PATHS CO

WHITNEY MCVEIGH

Paths Converge *Infinite Strange Shapes*
Prose, poems, drawings, photographs 1994-2025

SYLPH
EDITIONS

When thou art weary, on the mountains stay,
And when exhausted, drink the rivers' driven spray
(I.XIII.4-5)

from Kālidāsa's *Cloud Messenger*

Contents

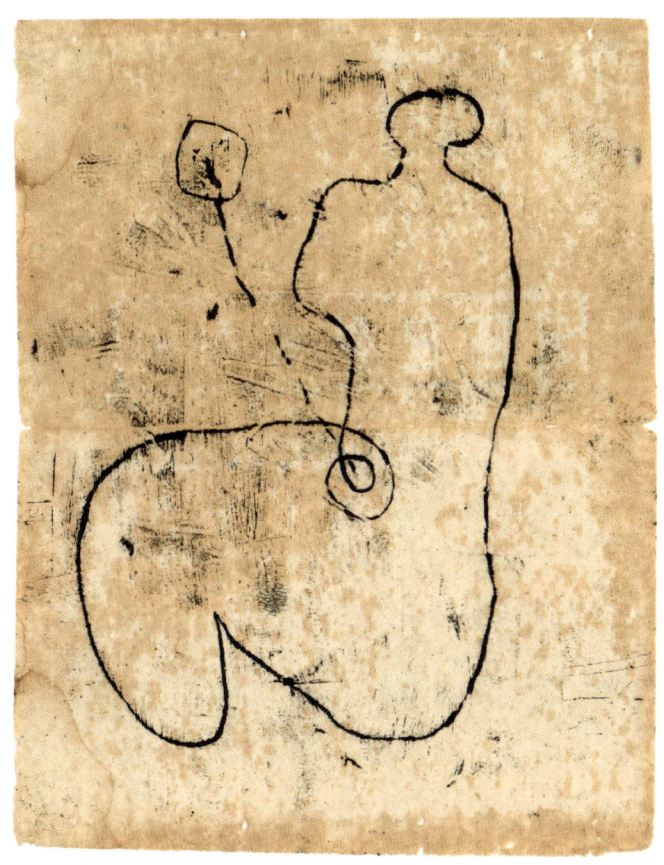

A BIRD-LIKE FORM, its wings are clipped, they appear like stunted arms. Its body made of wood punctured in places – an erosion of surfaces reminiscent of the earth. A long hollow rises from the centre of its wooden frame.

Who are you? A nemesis or fall, your weathered state reflecting the immensity of your journey. Once buried in the earth, the added weight of your history, you stand in silence. Your three-foot-high form is so far from the cold climes of your origins.

THERE ARE ROOFTOPS and shadows in the drawing by my mother, and a hill with trees in the background. The piece is divided by a line, as if she is perched low on a slope looking across to the village. On the left, there's a bell tower and a cracked facade, the street has drawn lines. The sunlight comes from the east, casting shadows across the houses and arched windows. There is no one in the picture, only the buildings and angular pines made of suggested lines.

IN THE PHOTOGRAPH above the desk, we are facing the camera. The fishing rod divides the frame. I have blue leather shoes on, jeans and a white T-shirt, I am five years old. There are stones on the ground between us and tumbleweed rising behind our heads. My hair is short and tied back on the right side. Baldwin is to the left. It's as if together we're holding something. His shoes are red and his shirt yellow. He is six years old.

By the open door is an antique bronze fork, about two feet high, with holes in the handle, once used for trapping fresh-water eels. Mounted on a stand, it's now a sculpture in my mother's house. The wind reaches it from the window, the sound adrift of memory.

The Children's Treasure House, 'the book of the changing year', is here in the library. The first volume titled 'Immortal heroes of the world'. The descriptive passages in the books for children have a tenderness to them. They offer a return to the wonder of childhood.

The shelves are otherwise empty now, aside from particles of dust that sometimes, with the smallest movement, reach to meet the sunlight.

I WAS RAISED IN NATURE and witnessed life's evanescence: a sense of impermanence in the constant cycles of the seasons. I grew up in a small village on the east coast of America. Here, in sub-zero winters, we ice-skated on lakes and made angels in the snow, leaving an imprint of our young lives.

An early childhood memory was of passing an abandoned car in the forest off the track that led to the Long Island Sound. You took the same route each time, the windows open to the smell of low shore and seaweed, driving towards the tidal estuary of the Atlantic Ocean. To the left in the distance was an old Volkswagen amidst the beech trees, with broken windows and clothes strewn in the moss-covered branches. We told each other stories about it, its mystery, I wonder now what its true history was. An object reveals itself through time and we picked up on something of its past as we drove to our swimming lessons.

THE LAST TIME I visited my mother's, the books on my bedside table were Albert Camus's *Selected Essays and Notebooks*, *The Oxford Book of Sea Stories*, P. G. Wodehouse's *Love Among the Chickens*, *Poems on the Underground* and Lee Rourke's *Everyday*. Literature has always informed and helped me through adversity. My mother gave me a short story by Saki over the few days there, 'The Open Window'. It was a tale of the vivid imagination of a child.

MY GRANDFATHER'S LIBRARY in Old Westbury was a small room with a bay window and inset shelves lined mainly with non-fiction: fly fishing and history. Above the fireplace was a perfectly preserved salmon, framed in a glass box. Salmon are anadromous fish; born in fresh water, they migrate to salt water, then return to fresh water to spawn. In Celtic mythology, the salmon is associated with wisdom. A fisherman, my grandfather spent much of his life on rivers. He told stories of the silence and mystery below the water, the waiting space and deep sense of time as he observed the movement of the water and trees.

There was a formality to my grandparents' house in Long Island. The scale of it was immense, with its sweeping staircase that transformed the central space, and extensive gardens of marigolds with a private burial place for the dogs. They had four Welsh corgis that followed us around the home and were the subject of laughter and joy.

LOCUST VALLEY, Long Island was a 'hamlet and census-designated place' located in Nassau County, New York, a small railroad town where people played country club sports and drank a lot.

Growing up, we climbed the steps of the high diving board, kept fireflies in jars, making lanterns at night, and did the ordinary things children do. We would stand in a circle, one foot in and one foot out, and prick our fingers, press them against each other's, becoming blood sisters and brothers, the ritual now complete. It was 1976, the year we left Long Island for England. I was seven years old and remember a sense of loss. It was around this time I made my first drawing on the cotton heart of a Raggedy Ann doll.

I BECAME INTERESTED in the archive through seeing a range of black and white photographs of my grandmother's marble sculptures on Long Island. I was struck by their subjects of ecology and by the light coming from a makeshift window in her studio. Around this time, I was given a small bag of clay that belonged to her. Her life ended prematurely when my mother was in her thirties. Dried out, like Callanish rock, the clay still sits in my studio window, wrapped in old newspaper. I often think about the imprint of my grandmother's hands in its surface. Like contours in the landscape, out of it emerges the luminosity of memory.

IN FRONT OF THE STUDIO is a building with steel slats dividing windows rising to the sky. From where I stand I can see at least a hundred windows, all exactly the same, with blue curtains. Everywhere I look for the sun but it's hidden.

The floor is covered in dust, small drawings on paper and boxes of all shapes filled with ordinary materials such as old photographs, newspapers, locks, keys, watches, records, letters, sheet music, children's clothes, ambrotypes, trade tools. On the table are objects from travel: stones, pieces of wood, clay, reference books, decks of cards, 1950s games, pots and pans, clock parts and sculptures made and found. My son's casts stand in the window. The walls are lined with books, mostly published before 1950, linen backed.

On a side table, wrapped around a branch found in our Somerset forest, is a fragment of sheet music with the words 'borders, countries; contemporary death-grapple'. A small sculpture in the making, 2014.

I REMEMBER READING about how the present disappears so quickly, it's as if one needs to move faster to hold on to it. An acceleration took place over the last ten years. It seems the past is full of mishaps belonging to other peoples's versions of events. My own stories are becoming clearer as they reveal themselves through the vast passage of time.

Excavation and Earth
How we come to live with the demands of modern life. Children, mothers, time – our rootedness to the earth and nature – the past informing the future – excavation and a constant questioning of the loss of self in modern life.

Preliminary Work
Foundations – growing up, introspection, education and the building of worlds through a medium.

Concrete
Our connection to ourselves and to the earth – the need to be attached to something as humans in order to remain. The ordinary and mundane, making poetry out of this.

Form
New concepts to describe the fundamental and our desires.
Creating form and accessing the unknown.

Reinforcement
Repetition in the ordinary both in language and gesture – finding faith and strength in collecting.

Masonry
The building blocks of existence and of raising children. Kitchen and the home, an inventory.

Waterproofing
How we protect all that we love from the world around us.

Roofing
Home and symbolism.

Carpentry and Joinery
Bolts and battles.

Sanitary Installation
Cleansing of the flood of others' imagery, a return to truth.

Electrical Work
Fixing to bring light.

IN 1974, I WAS FIVE YEARS OLD. We were sweeping leaves in our back garden in Locust Valley with my father. I remember the wheelbarrow, the large red tomatoes and the sound of his laughter. That year he'd bought a leaf blower. The garden was on a slope facing a low-level boarded shed with a glassless window. We'd take a running jump into the leaves that smelt of the earth. We sold the vegetables by the side of the road, my brother and I made 20 cents each. There were thunderstorms in summer months, we'd run naked through the rain, stamping in shallow puddles, and witnessed the light breaking.

SOMETHING HAPPENS TO A PAGE or an object when you remove it from its original context and isolate it. Its meaning transforms. I'm interested in a kind of constant renegotiation of identity through the lens of materials, objects and their histories. This idea of moving through, for example, working with ink in dialogue with the materials, letting the materials lead; the image forms itself in the making. It's the same principle with books and objects and isolated pages and drawings. There's a kind of inter-relationship in knowing, unknowing, visible versus invisible worlds. An inventory reads as a poem.

Below are books selected for the assemblage *Way of Life* at Mount Stuart in Scotland, whose library comprises 25,000 books:

Essays on Home Subjects
History of Voyages
Wild Life Across the World
Borlase's Natural History
A Treatise on Forest-Trees
Miller's Gardener's Dictionary
British Birds
Handy Book of the Flower Garden
The Miracle of the Human Body
A Voice Through a Cloud
Dictionary of Scientific Terms
The Desert Home
Enquire Within
How Things Are Made

Window, cloud, memory
Drive me to this place
Bustle is my name
Children in the white
Forming their own thoughts
Motherless for today

2008

HAPTIC MEMORY is 'the form of sensory memory specific to touch stimuli…used regularly when assessing the necessary forces for gripping and interacting with familiar objects.' It is memory formed through connection to tangible material. Even the drawn line itself becomes a vehicle for memory. Plato wrote about how in the course of our lives, we expand our knowledge through expanding the sensory imagination. We assimilate knowledge through association and we evolve. The question is, are we architects of our own memory? Is time something that can be recreated or reborn?

THE PAST OF EVERY INDIVIDUAL undergoes constant transformations in his or her memory, and more often than not it acquires the features of an irretrievable land made more and more strange by the flow of time.

CZESŁAW MIŁOSZ

A CHILD STANDS, unable to penetrate the loss of time. In the drawing, there is a fragment cut from a page of *The Children's Treasure House* years before, that reads:

'God made our bodies of all the dust that is scattered about the world, that we may wander in search of home.'

MORTON HOYNE is the name of the village in the dream. A hamlet in the north-west of the country at the foot of huge granite mountains that appear yellow and black. Descending, we see the pink facade of a 19th-century church. In front of it are women in traditional dress, their white skirts moving gently in the breeze.

Beyond the covered square is a dark, narrow passage; at the end, a room where we stay. We walk past market stalls offering ancient stones and tools, examples of local rock, and a small metal-framed window with sculptures of Highland cattle made of bronze by a local foundry. Through a doorway is a staircase to the lit room with a table where we eat. I am with a musician, singer and guide, and reminded of the walk to Petra I made years before, the faces of granite emerging as we descended from the mountain. Jung wrote about images existing in us before birth, and the landscape in Scotland, where my children were born, has always felt familiar.

WORDS, ENGLISH WORDS, are full of echoes, of memories, of associations – naturally. They have been out and about, on people's lips, in their houses, in the streets, in the fields for so many centuries. And that is one of the chief difficulties in writing them today – that they are so stored with meanings, with memories, that they have contracted so many famous marriages. The splendid word 'incarnadine', for example – who can use it without remembering also 'multitudinous seas'? ... Words belong to each other, although, of course, only a great writer knows that 'incarnadine' belongs to 'multitudinous seas' ... Our business is to see what we can do with the English Language ... How can we combine the old words in new orders so that they survive, so that they create beauty, so that they can tell the truth? That's the question.

VIRGINIA WOOLF

A WOODEN RIB of a boat found in the north-west of Scotland 25 years ago lies on the concrete floor of my studio. It has moved from home to home and more recently found its way back here. It seemed necessary to hold on to this. It relates to ships propelled by wind and Alan Villiers' stories behind his photographs at sea of long wind ship voyages. Sometimes there's a desire to understand what it is to have lived before and the wood, with its bent nails and frayed body, tells its own story.

THROUGH THE WINDOW there's a light that marks the sky. Threads are bound together in a kind of weave suspended low below the clouds. You may see it early morning or just before sunset.

Looking up, you will have a view of the Firth of Clyde, an inlet of the Atlantic Ocean off the south-west coast, named for the River Clyde which runs into it. Historically it was used as a trade route and is a place of natural beauty and history.

In the landscape there are sequoia trees from North America, plants from South America and Australasia and species from the southern hemisphere that flourish here. As you descend to the sea, you'll see 'soft ferns', tropical plants originating in Australia. A Highland Boundary Fault draws across Bute, separating the lowlands from the highlands. 'A fault is a fracture in the bedrock in which observable movement has taken place.'

There is a cave there by the sea. When you enter the light is dim. Last time we were there, I noticed inscribed on the wall: 'Doubt is a tower that closes to the sky, it's painted blue and commands us to listen. Like a humpback whale with outstretched wings, a never-ending story, passengers to other places.'

What is worthwhile doing in this world – to navigate, to expand, to imagine, to love, to find gateways in order to reach the truth? A form of cultivation takes place through our lives as we search for connections, to unlock further meaning. On the ceiling in the hall, Helen of Troy stands under the constellation known as the Northern Cross. In Greek mythology, it was said she hatched from a swan's egg and was known for her awakening and illumination of the soul. There are forty-nine constellations of the northern hemisphere here that reflect the sky in 1880, at the time when the house was built. Other women from myth and history are represented on the upper ceiling, surrounding the great hall.

Last night I stayed in the house. The rain came down until 3 a.m. and I was glad to wake to sunlight and trees. Standing on the lawn, I see the clouds moving in again and I will, like you, leave this place soon.

These white marks pictu are bright lists of books

THERE IS A BLUE LINEN-BACKED BOOK in my studio found in a second-hand shop in Krugersdorp, South Africa. Scattered around the store were various plastic objects, piles of old newspapers and, up on a shelf, a small hard-backed book. Inside was a note from a man to a woman about the spiritual qualities of nature alongside photographs of trees. She had gone out and found leaves from the same trees and placed them inside. The preface of the book reads, 'It is possible to gather gold, where it may be had, with moonlight. This book is written to any who are walking in difficult places and who care to gather that gold.' The work is a window into a woman's life, it was published in the UK in 1937 and yet made the journey to South Africa. It speaks of the ordinary intimate spaces we create in order to remember.

IT TOOK SEVEN MONTHS to create the radial poem *Towards the Light*, commissioned by Mount Stuart in Scotland. In the centre is a moon; the lines of the poem, etched into brass, fan out from there. Brass is often used for labelling outdoor sculptures and for memorials in churches; in the work this traditional use is contrasted with contemporary text.

The poem reflects on our connection to the universe and how we document the passing of time. It considers how we create new visions of history from the past itself. A reinvention of a radial poem from the Mount Stuart archive, I've adapted an historical artefact for the present moment, creating a canto, a voice for the future. These astronomical and temporal themes are echoed in the design of the Horoscope Room at Mount Stuart. The poem is written in vernacular English. The first letter of each line forms the title, 'What Is Worthwhile Doing In This World. What Will It Profit A Man If He Gain The Whole World And Suffer The Loss of his Soul.'

IN FREUD'S *Civilization and Its Discontents*, there's a section on the 'conservation of the mind' where he says, 'Everything survives in some way or other, and is capable under certain conditions of being brought to light again'.

In 2016, I buried a cross given to me in Ethiopia underneath an arrangement of stones made in the landscape in South Africa. In Ethiopian Christian Orthodox tradition, the cross encompasses the life of the world in both its macrocosmic and microcosmic dimensions. Last time I was there, the long grass prevented me from finding it.

It's winter now and the site is located up in the reserve, formerly an inland sea. The silver cross was buried for two years. The image is what remains of a woman's arrangement of stones in the earth.

ALONG THE YELLOW RIVER is a blue boat with an oar leaning on the edge, pointing to the sky. Below it is a box with scribbled marks of umber paint inside. A tree rises to the left, uncertain in its reach. The composition is blue-brown, cadmium yellow with layers of bone black. Underneath the boat, on the near side, is a shadow of a blue bird. The painting is titled *The Yellow River*.

I AM READING AN ESSAY by Deleuze and Guattari that looks at the 'perpetual flux of all things', the idea not of things in a world but of things becoming things and the world becoming a world. That we 'make things visible' rather than recreate what's there. John Berger alluded to this idea when he observed that there's no inside or outside and no boundary separating them. We extend along multiple trails and this can sometimes lead to chaos, an 'expression of an inner space' and 'an openness to the world'. Every object I work with takes on meaning, has a life of its own and can trigger an association. The line itself is a vehicle for memory.

EXHIBITED AT MOUNT STUART HOUSE are four letters written by children to their mother, selected from the Mount Stuart archive. Carefully framed, they hang in the bathroom. Next door, in the bedroom, are two ink on paper drawings of a mother and child drawn whilst there, based on early photographs from the archive.

Motherhood is represented here as an intimate and universal experience. There is a life-long process for a mother and child, a need for separation and a longing to return – it is in these letters, handwritten by children, some accompanied by small drawings. The children, living on a small island, long for the boat to come to the harbour. The bath is a place of solace for a mother, yet the voices of our children – past, present, future – stay with us always.

THE *Oracle Enquiry* is an essay that was formed a long time ago. It looks at the infrastructure of poetry, a future library that would contain not only books and archive material but paintings and drawings that speak collectively, an intuitive accruing of material over time and the unfolding narratives of human histories. Sometimes a photograph or an object belonging to a person speaks deeply of time and of my own experience. There's a sense in arranging of waiting to be shown what the material brings.

To WRITE A POEM is to attempt a minor magic. The instrument of that magic, language, is mysterious enough. We know nothing of its origin. We know only that it divides into diverse lexicons and that each one of them comprises an indefinite and changing vocabulary and an undefined number of syntactic possibilities. With those evasive elements I have formed this book. (In the poem, the cadence and atmosphere of a word can weigh more than its meaning.)

This book is yours, Maria Kodama. Must I say to you that this inscription includes twilights, the deer of Nara, night that is alone and populated mornings, shared islands, seas, deserts, and gardens, what forgetting loses and memory transforms, the high-pitched voice of the muezzin, the death of Hawkwood, some books and engravings?

We can only give what we have given. We can only give what is already the other's. In this book are things that were always yours. How mysterious a dedication is, a surrender of symbols!'

JORGE LUIS BORGES

Dear friends of the sky,
I am waiting for the stars.
My skin is a slow molecule of fiction,
My bones,
A widening crevice.
This body is a house,
The light filters through today.

2024

THE INSTALLATION *Divine Rules* began with a conversation with a curator and a collection of books given to me by my mother. The prefaces of these books reflect widely on life and are written in a way that is personal to the author. This initial collection sat in my studio for years. The library, mostly collected in the UK, grew over time to encompass nine hundred books.

In the library are books on engineering, mathematics, physics, ship-building, telegraphy, astronomy, home-keeping, nature, geology, time, language, genealogy – all subjects that in some way unify us as humans. The books were published before the internet, mostly before 1950.

The concept for the library was to create a space of universal knowledge through the exhibiting of books and to convey the idea of a living collective language based on shared references. The books in this collection act as symbols or souls, vehicles to expand the imagination – both through the physical nature and age of the objects and the knowledge contained inside. The titles are arranged to provoke thinking through association: *Feminine Frailty* sits next to *Man the World Over*. Juxtaposition starts a new conversation. The library was formed intuitively and seeks to remind us of all that connects us, that fundamentally we share human values and the need to learn in order to expand our lives.

The philosophy of Plato forms the intellectual thread that runs through the work. Plato saw artists and craftspeople as producers of images that reside in the realm of thought. Similar to Carl Jung, he believed that to learn truth is the soul remembering what it learned before birth, and that the 'exercise of our senses upon sensible objects' is a way of reclaiming that knowledge. The books in the library can be seen as 'images' or 'sensible objects' that light the path to knowledge and truth. The library as a whole can be approached as a composition, a metaphor for truth, the books acting as beacons.

In Plato's *Phaedo*, before Socrates is forced to die, he refers to a dream in which he's told to make music. He identifies the study of philosophy with the pursuit of life and extols it as 'the noblest and best of music'. In the end, he composes a piece that will live on beyond his death. Socrates sees the soul as the purest form of truth and describes sight and hearing and the physical body as 'inaccurate witnesses'.

Death then is the ultimate truth, a transcending of the physical with all of its limitations. Yet in our lifetimes we rely on the physical to trigger and enable the creation of stories. The library remains closed: visitors can approach, but cannot open the books. In this way it suggests the gap between physical and transcendental, visible and invisible. Books, physical objects, are like portals to intangible worlds – ideas, stories, truth and knowledge which exist between the covers.

Toward the end of *Phaedrus*, Socrates introduces the origins of writing through the god Theuth. Again the debate is on the truth of the soul, in this case the 'living' word being superior to the written word. One could argue that in the modern world we are frequently recording and documenting and not necessarily 'experiencing'.

The books' silence can be challenging, but equally can unlock the imagination, enabling us to see further into dimensionless spaces, into life, truth, meaning, knowledge itself. The library remains closed but we are witnesses to its history.

DRAWING IS A WAY of discovering limitless space and spatial time. I remember as a child staring at the wallpaper, seeing infinite variations of the same flower. To draw is to re-evaluate or find life through the line itself. Just as each blade of grass is different, each line carries its history and the life of the person from whom it comes. As a professor once said, every signature is individual, written from the hand of an individual. He also said there's no light without dark and no dark without light. The flower was a repeated design but my eyes saw an ever-evolving world.

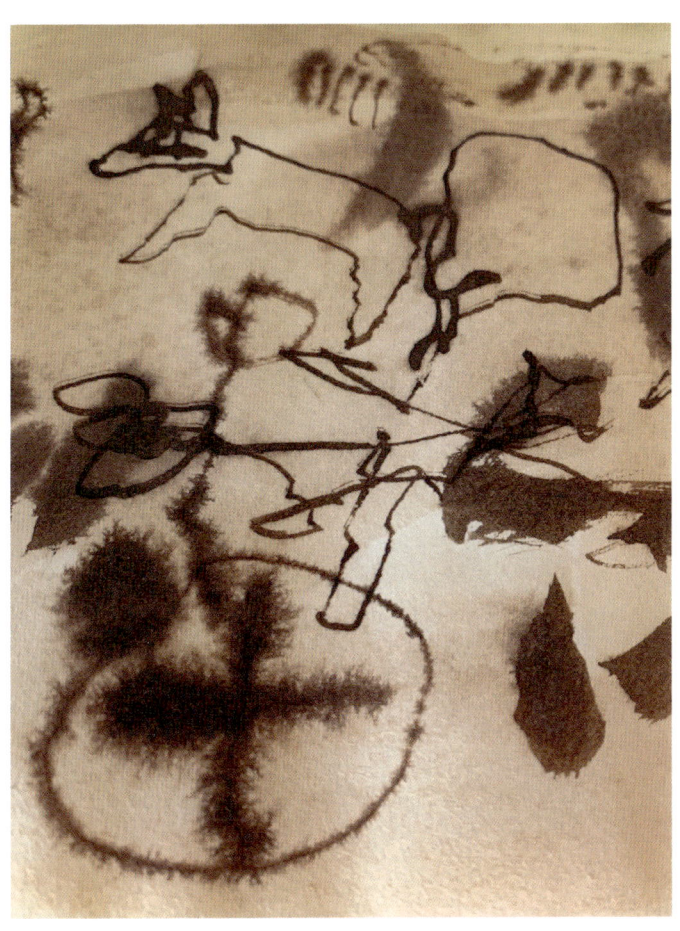

IN MY BOOK there are photographs of Palmyra. The ancient city began as a small settlement near the Efqa spring on the southern bank of Wadi al-Qubur. It was first recorded in the early second millennium BCE and grew wealthy from trade caravans, renowned merchants who established colonies along the Silk Road. The first image is the Valley of the Tombs – these descend underground. The last is the view taken from the 13th-century castle Qala'at ibn Maan, looking down over Palmyra. It was 103 degrees in the desert that day and only a few people were there.

On the last day in Damascus, in June 2009, sitting with a bookseller in his small shop, he opened up a door at the back to a library that had belonged to his grandfather. It was the first time I became conscious of a library as a construct of memory.

HARDLY ANY BOOKS published before 1950 are left in my library at home. One is a smallish green-coloured hardback titled *Alfred, Lord Tennyson, A Memoir by his Son*, published in 1897. On opening the book I discovered a portrait of Tennyson, whose work I'd first read thirty years before. It contains fragments, letters, tributes and stories. The others are *The Children's Treasure House* and Katherine Mansfield's *Journals*, found in New York in the '90s. All of the other books are gone now, having made their way to America.

> But now farewell. I am going a long way
> With these thou seëst – if indeed I go –
> (For all my mind is clouded with a doubt)
> To the island-valley of Avilion;
> Where falls not hail, or rain, or any snow,
> Not ever wind blows loudly; but it lies
> Deep-meadow'd, happy, fair with orchard-lawns
> And bowery hollows crown'd with summer sea,
> Where I will heal me of my grievous wound.
>
> ALFRED, LORD TENNYSON

IN THE MUSEUM, there's a small opening in a wall to look through, where they have recreated José Saramago's office furnished with an old typewriter, reference books and collected sculptures. His library of 16,000 books is in Lanzarote where he died. The notes say, 'He gathered because he wanted to share his intellectual and literary labour with the craftsman, or the worker or the peasant, aware that in life, as citizens, we all must be equally judged and that our creative work, sensibility and effort will be valued by others.'

José Saramago died on 18 June 2010 at his home on the island. When the plane that would bring him back to Lisbon was about to take off, his neighbours came out onto the streets to read aloud fragments of the books he wrote on the island: so with the sound of the words he created, he left Lanzarote. Upon arriving in Lisbon, others, also his readers, were waiting for him, raising books to the sky, saying, 'The books carry within a person, the author.'

Saramago's epitaph is the last sentence of his novel *Memorial do Convento*: 'But did not ascend to the stars, for it belonged to the earth.'

PETRA IS ONE OF THE MOST MYSTERIOUS and spiritual landscapes I've encountered. There are caves and carvings, prayer places dedicated to the presence of Dussehra. The Nabateans, a nomadic people from north-western Arabia, came here between the sixth and fourth centuries BCE. It was built at the intersection of the Silk Route which connected India and China with Egypt and the Hellenistic world, and the incense route from Arabia to Damascus. My guide Ismael took me on an ancient route to the mountain, away from the hub of people – we descended into the ancient city, sometimes bent like creatures, climbing through the rock.

ARTHUR RIMBAUD'S *Illuminations* is a book I frequently travel with. In Ethiopia, I made a pilgrimage of sorts to the city of Harar, where he lived for a time. Built between the 13th and 16th centuries, the ancient part of the city is a warren of small colourful cobbled streets. One is solely for tailors, all working outside. The museum and house dedicated to Rimbaud's work is timeless, with wooden balconies and latticed windows. I had a conversation there with the curator about poetry as a means to uncover life's truths. That day, he loaned me a first edition of *Illuminations* from the library.

DEPARTURES

Enough seen. The vision has been encountered in all skies.
   Enough had. Sounds of cities, in the evening, and in sunlight, and always.
   Enough known. The stations of life. — O Sounds and Visions!
   Departure amid new noise and affection!

ARTHUR RIMBAUD

IN RIMBAUD'S *Illuminations*, we read of 'Temples lit up by returning processions, immense vistas of the fortification of modern coastlines; dunes illustrated with warm flowers and bacchanals; grand canals of Carthage...' Scholars have tried to retrace Rimbaud's steps because of the diversity of places mentioned, some of which they think he hadn't been to. I retraced his steps in Harar last year. I developed a fever there at the time of reading the poems and was taken back to that time. It was as if I was transported, wandering the painted city with its endless passageways, understanding the path to wisdom as sacred.

THERE ARE FOOTPRINTS and drawings in the desert in Wadi Rum in Jordan where travellers have been walking for centuries. Almost all the people living here are of Bedouin origins and traditionally led nomadic lives. When you are in this landscape, there's a sense of an echo of history and an overwhelming sense of the breadth of time. The sand patterns and rock formations are like no others I've ever seen. There are markers of human settlements along the way and indications of trade routes.

In 2017, I visited the archaeological site in Madaba during a research trip to Zaatari Refugee Camp, home to 79,000 Syrian refugees. The northern part of the city contains mosaics dating back to the Byzantine-Umayyad period and crosses a colonnaded Roman road, some of which still exists, with a church and crypt dating back to 600 CE. A sixth-century mosaic map of Jerusalem and the Holy Land is there. Roman columns and stones were often reused for Byzantine and Islamic structures later. The city is located 30 km south-west of Amman along a road known as the King's Highway. One of the most beautiful mosaics is the Tree of Life.

TONIGHT IS THE 'HARVEST MOON', a term coined before
electricity when farmers depended on light at night. It is the nearest
full moon to the autumnal equinox. I woke with the sensation of
a pull to and weight of consciousness. For a few nights around
this time our satellite rises early, illuminating the night sky and
making it easier for farmers to continue harvesting their crops
after sundown.

TODAY I SAW A BIRD flying low in a valley in the mountains. The mystery of nature unfolded unexpectedly in those moments of flight. Time suspended, wings held by indefinable air and light. We watched it soar, marking spaces and places that will never belong to us. Nature, momentary and present where creatures are free to roam. We stopped to observe, its wings appeared small and black.

IN 2017, I VISITED XUANKONG TEMPLE on Hengshan mountain in northern China, suspended and small to the scale of the mountain, a beautiful and understated feat of architecture. Built in 491, high up in the mountains, to laws of Taoism so all noise would drop away, it is the only existing temple to include Buddhism, Taoism and Confucianism. It is made of wood and stilts and has survived more than 1,500 years. The inside has been preserved as it was. Created by abseiling across the mountain face, it's one of the most astonishing places I've visited, illustrating humans' faith in nature and the immensity, silence and vastness of the universe and sky.

IN A SMALL 18TH-CENTURY ROOM in Ouro Preto, Brazil,
14 standing sculptures were on the ornate wooden desk, all covered
in dust. Men and women disguised as saints, carved in wood with
brittle robes of red and blue, worn down over the years. There's
a man with a crown, his hands clasped in prayer. A mirror is
suspended behind the group, the dust fades the reflection, creating
a fragile sense of time.

Later, I visited the church of St Francis of Assisi. On the wall in
the crypt is a painting of a four-poster bed with red curtains. A boy
is asleep under ochre sheets. Beside the bed, a cloud hovers like a
metaphor and inside it a woman holds her hands in her lap with
eight swords crossing her chest. My own hands are clasped as I
take this in. The board is blue, representing the sky. Below it is an
inscription that includes the date, 1775. The painting is on a small
wooden fragment.

THE OCEANIC FIGURE, made of stone, stands poised on the shelf at home, his feet disappearing into the grey slab beneath. His arms are curled inwards as if to wrap across his chest. Around the neck is a scarred series of lines suggesting a body piece. His frame is rectangular and his cheeks are sunken, the marks of tools visible in his eyes. His double-sided form suggests the inside and outside of our lives.

CURSIVE STRUCTURES like fallen trees with branches form the foundations of a painting.

THE PERFORMANCE OF INK ON PAPER: the emergence of movement and existential paths into memory; a discourse of mind and materials as the ink lies bare on the page. The force of bone black fractured by light; a crack in the infrastructure of a kind of deep time-field, an elegy to nature. Here: sage, Dadhichi's bones, dust, carbon, water, deity, Indra, myth, sky, shadow, time, presence, memory.

MY MEMORIES sometimes change and lose or gain strength depending on the scale of them. My children are grown now and unquantifiable; they shine like stars. Wherever I stand I see them. Time, how we experience it and attempt to hold it. It seems only days ago they were young; they are now the age I was when I met their father.

THESE ARE THIN PLACES: a veil between the physical and spiritual world.

They invite a heightened consciousness, an opening up to all that is possible.

Reflect in the light,
A counterpart to faith.
This roadless travel,
Imminent freedom,
Sacred day.

2016

THE ARMS ARE ELONGATED at the top, with smaller forearms. Hands, fingers spread, rest on the lower belly where the wood swells into a womb or bodily tomb. The woman's pose is one of reticence, a large scar runs across the centre of the body, the linear grooves of identity or religious status reminiscent of an opening. The wood is dappled and worn underneath a black matt paint that's flaking to the orange colour of what appears to be the original fruit wood. The eyes are sad, cast down, carved simply. Though graphic, it's intensely human and stands on a small piece of wood in my room.

THE SEA SWELLS and turns, beckons with its deep dark hues of greys and blacks. The enchanting light and clarity of an underworld sits below the surface.

THE YELLOW RIBBON floats from the deer's head and points towards the sky. He remains on the west side of the river, where the mountain provides solace and shadow. The sky is pale blue and pink, two birds soar at an even pace. If you close your eyes, all you hear is the sound of water and wind. This is a recurring dream; somewhere is the moving water, where paintings lie of all I've imagined and made over the years.

An omnibus of creation,
In the thinking space of time.
Burial site,
Proposition,
Human social ritual.
A walk, a march,
A requiem to freedom.

2019

THE WAVES MARK A DAY I will remember when the sun collided with the stars and the world lapsed momentarily into darkness – we turned to find the sea and a great swell came.

A ruin stands,
And holds a memory,
Our combined history.

Silence ripples,
Particles elope,
Circle our common places,
Hold us close,
Take our dreams.

A building aches,
Yesterday's sound,
Does he remember?

A blade of grass,
Fragile in the rain,
Bends to the sun,
Whispers a name.

I will become everything
Always and what I was
For this one time
Here
Now and
Then

2023

WHEN I WAS YOUNG, I read John Berger's work and I have kept returning to it. In his writing, he makes references to the 'continent of the physical', the idea of mapping territory through the body. Over the years, I've understood this as a way of finding new spaces through intuitive methods, in response to nature. The work comes from somewhere else, yet it's also from within and uncovers maps that can only be located through memory and the landscape's memory. Jung believed images exist in us before we are born and perhaps it is a task in this lifetime to draw these out through a medium. I work with spaces and time and pre-existing matter. Like all of life, everything passes, has an end and we are left with traces. We form through remembering.

WHAT DO WE SEE? Thyme, other shrubs, limestone rocks, olive trees on a hillside, in the distance a plain, in the sky birds. He dips the pen into brown ink, watches, and marks the paper. The gestures come from his hand, his wrist, arm, shoulder, perhaps even the muscles in his neck, yet the strokes he makes on the paper are following currents of energy which are not physically his and which only become visible when he draws them. Currents of energy? The energy of a tree's growth, of a plant's search for light, of a branch's need for accommodation with its neighbouring branches, of the roots of thistles and shrubs, of the weight of rocks lodged on a slope, of the sunlight, of the attraction of the shade for whatever is alive and suffers from the heat, of the Mistral from the north which has fashioned the rock strata. My list is arbitrary; what is not arbitrary is the pattern his strokes make on the paper. The pattern is like a fingerprint. Whose?

JOHN BERGER

PERHAPS ONE DAY you might consider the idea of a place of history and culture represented through objects and books. I'm not sure what else matters, aside from the things that belong to us or hold meaning. Yesterday I spent the afternoon in a bookshop in Kyoto. There's an accident that occurred in one of the books, an ink spill that appears like a Rorschach test between two pages. It has spread its wings and is beautiful. I later discovered that the book is an encyclopaedia of a woman's life. There are other books of poetry that I bought for very little, some two hundred years old, all in calligraphy. What's interesting is that in the absence of any understanding of language there's a sense of what the material yields. It begins a thought process around the line being the poem itself. Which is in fact how I make all of my work.

In the same way, there have been people whom I've become friends with in the absence of language. I experienced it today for the first time in years in Kyoto with a 94-year-old woman whose *ryokan* I stayed in. We talked to one another, I couldn't understand, yet we shared something and we both knew. It's only happened a handful of times. At the end of our conversation she walked over to an old chest and pulled some papers from a drawer, words in translation. She leafed through them and held one to her forehead, 'you are wonderful.'

THE ARTIST FROM KOSOVO talked about an important archive. In many ways my thoughts are around an archive that's universal and belongs to us all; an archive that gives emphasis to ordinary but valuable histories, whether it takes the form of a library or another kind of cultural space. In my studio there are fragments that speak to and about the lives of others. They are also a protest against the loss of time; this is why I collect and have collected and recorded for many years.

TODAY I FOUND Katherine Mansfield's *Journals*, published in 1933, in which she describes an experience of the body, similar to one I had in regard to a dream. It relates to something I read by Deleuze on Spinoza about man defined as territory, that we only have ourselves as our own territory, that we can expand and limit ourselves through this territory.

The juxtaposition of text and image, and taking text and books out of context and placing them in new arrangements and contexts (including the domestic), forms a different kind of language. This is what I'm suggesting, through a library, and through found material, pages, etc. In the young person's library book introduction that's here, one of the lines says, 'The imagination is always making a larger and better world than that which we see.'

Solitude

Solitude is like a rain
That from the sea at dusk begins to rise;
It floats remote across the far-off plain
Upward into its dwelling-place, the skies,
Then o'er the town it slowly sinks again.
Like rain it softly falls at that dim hour
When ghostly lanes turn toward the shadowy morn;
When bodies weighed with satiate passion's power
Sad, disappointed from each other turn;
When men with quiet hatred burning deep
Together in a common bed must sleep –
Through the gray, phantom shadows of the dawn
Lo! Solitude floats down the river wan...

RAINER MARIA RILKE

I WAS REFLECTING on the word 'illuminations' and it occurred to me that it could be beautiful to do a show where fragments of text are illuminated in the dark. The words themselves made of light. Their scale and presentation could allude to early illuminated manuscripts. And perhaps a library could be built out of the archives of other libraries.

THE ARTIST IN HIS SEVENTIES in Kyrgyzstan, who passed away, sang a song, 'I'll bring back a melody from my youth.' Something happened in that country, I saw people for who they were and the land as I've never seen it before.

IT WAS A BEAUTIFUL DRIVE across the highland plateaus of the Amhara region of North Ethiopia to see the eleven monolithic churches. Carved out of one piece of stone, the churches of Lalibella are large architectural feats, some of them level with the mountain. They remain a major site of Ethiopian Christian worship and pilgrimage.

A thousand years ago, we walked like covered shadows in the early morning darkness. Arriving on the edge of a steep incline, we watched a ceremony of priests gather, pray, play music, march and whisper, their bodies pressed closely to walls made of earth. The drums produced a guttural sound that reverberated through the rain-filled valley.

FROM LALIBELLA, it took five hours by car to reach the small weaving community of Awra Amba. I was immediately led into the visitors' centre, a small building surrounded by oak trees. On the walls of the centre were the community's rules for living, written by hand, together with the overall philosophy of founder Zumra Nuru. Now in his seventies, he had laid the foundations of this community over forty years before, having spent his early years championing the rights of women, children and the elderly. In 1972, disillusioned by what he felt was lacking in his own community, he met two people from neighbouring villages who shared his ideals and established Awra Amba. The village has grown outwards from its main square, where a large oak tree stands.

There is a building for the elderly, painted blue. A rectangular space with small cubicle-like rooms with blue curtains. The women, some having lived a century, are well taken care of and the aesthetics of living have been carefully thought out. This is a resting place where the women are cared for by the village.

ARRIVING IN SÃO RAIMUNDO in Piauí, Brazil, I was greeted by Rosa, a short woman in her sixties, with cropped hair and a cigarette perched on her lips. We drove to Sítio do Mocó, a small village that sits at the foot of the Serra da Capivara, a national park that spans 1,300 square kilometres. Despite my earlier research, nothing prepared me for the landscape and large rock formations, the sky and strange atmosphere of this village. Off the main road, it was a four-kilometre drive along a red dusty track, through farms, homesteads and a barrier into the village to the derelict school. Along the way there were cactuses that seemed to belong to another time.

Rosa showed me to a small room with a broken-tiled ceiling open to the exposed beams and sky. It was clean, the bed hard, old and leaning to one side. The room was one of six closed rooms on a terrace of the former school, with the ladies' bathroom and shower cubicles at the end. They had cleaned one of the cubicles for me, the rest were full of debris, dead insects, red earth and old newspapers. On turning on the tap in the sink, a rusty fluid poured out. Earlier, in London, I'd been informed that I was staying in a house in the national park.

There was a sense of absence and loss about the place. The concrete block of a school was surrounded by barbed wire on a high wall to keep out wild dogs, chickens and the puma at night. There were unfinished paintings of hunters on the cracked walls. I learned later that the mountain tigers had eaten many of the local animals and dogs and there was an overall sense of the wild at sunset; this is when the animals and insects emerged from their hidden spaces.

Rosa left with a younger Brazilian man who spoke no English. I was exhausted from two flights and travel from Salvador and a five-hour drive in a rental car, the first time I'd driven in South America. I had a small white Fiat that, like myself, seemed to take on the mountain landscape over the coming weeks, slowly eroding and becoming the colour of the dust. The sun was setting and I unpacked in this small room that had a sombre feeling of death about it.

Out of nowhere that evening appeared a young French archaeologist, part of a team who were staying nearby in another part of the school. They were inviting me to dinner. He was hovering, swaying on his feet as if suspended, there was a strong smell of alcohol and sweat that seemed to emanate from his body. I felt a sense of anticipation and relief as I ventured into the other part of the camp. I'd been travelling since three in the morning.

The table was roughly cut planks at the centre of the former schoolyard. There were twelve men, some seated around the table drinking beer, others preparing food. There was an edge to them that was uncomfortable. They'd been there for three months excavating the landscape, their minds fragile – there was touch of hysteria about the place. Occasionally one would roar with a guttural laughter that seemed to reverberate as if from across a thousand years.

The night was dense with stars. It was then I first spoke to French archaeologist Eric about the land and its memory. The idea that we seek out human traces in the landscape. A kind of furrowing and uncovering, like marks in the forest, we look for clues that lead us to the first line of enquiry. He was a large man with a full head of hair and facial hair who'd spent much of his life digging the earth. His eyes carried the weight of history beyond his years that I recognized. He saw me that night, it was a moment that would last forever.

Eric's team informed me over dinner that the *barbeiro* insect was active and tended to be in villages where there are farm animals and clay houses. Two of the younger men had been bitten and would be tested when back home. The insect is a small beetle with red marks on its back. Known as the kissing insect, it bites the face at night and carries a virus that has a one in three chance of killing you. It then takes ten years to die, as the virus slowly consumes your heart. I was sitting at the table when I heard this and later, with the wild of the night, an open ceiling and no net in my room, I experienced the arrival of a new kind of fear.

I moved to a *pousada* the following day, where I spent the remaining weeks of my trip – a small room protected from the night in Brazil. It took me a week to recover and I'd been bitten by all manner of creatures.

An artist's life is one that leads us to the valley from the mountain, where there is a constant reassessment before returning. I've travelled all over the world and have had experiences that will be logged forever, but to experience life so fully sometimes comes at a cost.

For the first time in Brazil I wondered if I could take this on.

LOCATED IN THE LEFT WING of the Luz monastery, the Museum of Sacred Art in São Paulo is a religious institution founded in 1774 by Frei Galvão. A long walk that took me through intrepid spaces today.

THE LEARNED DOCTORS of the Great Vehicle teach us that the essential characteristic of the universe is its emptiness. They are certainly correct with respect to the tiny part of the universe that is this book. Gallows and pirates fill its pages, and that word iniquity strikes awe in its title, but under all the storm and lightning, there is nothing. It is all just appearance, a surface of images – which is why readers may, perhaps, enjoy it. The man who made it was a pitiable sort of creature, but he found amusement in writing it; it is to be hoped that some echo of that pleasure may reach its readers.

JORGE LUIS BORGES

I WAS IN A STUDIO full of unfinished sculptures and in my pocket found my own small clay figures. I placed them on the table, they were not yet fired and slightly crumbling. As I walked down corridors filled with more strange figurines, I came across a door and pushed it open. The room was full of wet clay and water, like a beautiful rugged and open landscape. In the next space was the bedroom, people came here to stay. It seems every time I touched the small figures, they would fall apart even more. A kind man appeared and rearranged them so they had a semblance of order. The studio was in another country but before I could place it, the dream was over.

THE VAN IS PAINTED BLUE, there's cracked paint around the glassless window frame. Where the windshield wipers were is a radio antenna. The side door is open and slightly bent and rusted. There are red and white umbrellas in the distance, shielding those curled under them from the sun. Surrounding the frame of the vehicle are a furrow of rolled wire with a circular pattern, blue plastic bags, woven baskets, an orange toy frame for a child-walker and an old suitcase. On top is a metal frame secured to its body and in it a black hose, a piece of rope, knotted string, a child's scooter and a wheelbarrow. Locals say it's been parked there for years. The landscape is barren and the hills brown, dusty and dry in the 40 degree heat, with sounds of bleating. My children and I are at the foot of the easternmost slope. Everywhere I look I see abandoned clothes and shoes.

America, birthplace, 2015
Stone cold heart
Cabinet cards
Paper making
Glue

A rusted safety pin attaches,
Eye of the storm today.
A winged bird
Swells,
Dips,
Rises,
Conquers,
A configuration,
Sacred, immense.

2016

THE LETTERS IN THE BOX spoke of our years together.
The loss of time, an event in family history.

Here a painter
Below the sea,
An aggravated voice,
A wounding of space.
A chink in the light
Verifies the day.

1994

There is no vocabulary for failure there
Only a whisper,
A bird in flight,
A possible dream.

How did she know
That it would all
Be painted the
Colour of shadowed snow.

How did she know
It would come to this,
And that the colour
Would remain,
As pigment does on the skin.

How did she know
The world was blue
And that the flowers bore
Nothing but their own light.

2004

I TALKED THIS EVENING with an old friend of 25 years, about poetry and fiction as communication. In the same way a writer follows the language, the painter follows the line. We spoke about how important it is to say things we don't quite understand as artists and of inhabiting language, or paintings, essentially finding a place to live in the medium.

Time, immortal, flows like the river,
Crowned, orange, etched terracotta moon

Time, bound, eclectic, liminal,
The shadow of light, a bird in flight

You returned there, to the ocean shore and broken shell,
Sought silence in the woods

And history littered nearby trees of November gold,
Shaded by the summer months, centuries old

Shaped symbols belong to the sea floor,
Your inscription from a thousand years before

Under branches, tucked in ruffled pages and pinpoint leaves,
That match the image of those trees

Swelling in the salty heat,

You returned for the sky (an unwanted sigh),
Formless, spineless

Still as the swallow flies.

2022

I THINK A GREAT DEAL of my future and (how to) settle what book I am to write – how I shall re-form the novel and capture multitudes of things at present fugitive, enclose the whole, and capture infinite strange shapes. I take a good look at woods in the sunset, and fix men who are breaking stones with an intense gaze, meaning to sever them from past and future...but tomorrow I know, I shall be sitting down to the inanimate old phrases...

VIRGINIA WOOLF

AFTERWORD

.

SEVEN YEARS AGO an event took place that created a great upheaval in my life. It was during this time that I began to sift through fragments of writing – poems, journal entries and letters accumulated over the course of thirty years. Note-taking has always accompanied my practice as an artist, helping to ground the work in personal history and understand its relationship to a broader complex of ideas. Like drawing, it provided a way of cultivating and transporting, staying open to what a medium brings. This book is the result of bringing together these writings, alongside works on paper and photographs – themselves a kind of visual note-taking. Informed by my observations of the archive, I embraced the idea of the fragment, working to arrange, select and develop without striving for an illusion of completion. Woven through the book are letters to a curator and an account of the building of a library that took ten years.

As I looked back through all the work, I began to see a lifelong commitment to the imagination and the mystery of the unknown. The texts deal especially with memory and with landscapes and physical spaces. They try, through different approaches, to access these elusive arenas of human experience, whether near or far, trusting in processes as a way of acquiring metaphysical truths. Working in Asia and South Africa over twenty years, I gained a wider understanding of spiritual practices and the role of oral histories and storytelling. These traditions have shaped my work, guiding me in indexing universal human truths, connecting them through memory and association; finding ways to see.

Poetry has been an important means of taking stock and of documenting or recording events. As a mother of two children in the '90s, writing poems and drawing became like anchors, honest methods of accessing the moment and truth through the imagination. In amongst the pages are selected writings by artists and writers whose work has helped to navigate the challenges of this journey. They offer another way of entering that ephemeral space or moment – before the ink falls or a line is made – that holds something towards finding where the light is.

Valence, September 2025

List of images

Notes and references

p. 5   Kālidāsa, *Meghadūta* (*Cloud-messenger*), translated by Arthur W. Ryder, in *Shakuntala and Other Writings* (first published 1912)

p. 13   *The Children's Treasure House*, edited by Arthur Mee (London: Educational Book Company, 1925)

p. 17   'Locust Valley, New York', Wikipedia (last modified 2 August 2025)

p. 25   'Haptic memory', Wikipedia (last modified 26 May 2024)

p. 26   'Czesław Miłosz on Josef Koudelka's *Exiles*', ASX (9 June 2009), americansuburbx.com/2009/06/theory-czeslaw-milosz-on-josef.html

p. 30   Virginia Woolf quoted in Frances Spalding's *Virginia Woolf: Art, Life and Vision* (London: National Portrait Gallery, 2014), p. 146

p. 34   Originally titled *Dear Reader*, etched brass plate, 112 × 76cm, part of the author's solo exhibition *What is Worthwhile Doing in This World*, Mount Stuart Visual Arts, Bute, Scotland, 2019

p. 36   Amy Carmichael, *Gold by Moonlight* (1937)

p. 38   Sigmund Freud, *Civilization and Its Discontents*, translated by Joan Riviere (London: Hogarth Press, 1930), p. 15

p. 44   Jorge Luis Borges, *Selected Poems*, edited by Alexander Coleman (Penguin, 2000), p. 461

p. 46   Adapted from an interview with the author in Donatien Grau's *Plato in LA: Contemporary Artists' Visions*, published to accompany the exhibition of the same name at the J. Paul Getty Museum at the Getty Villa, 18 April to 3 September 2018

p. 52 Excerpt from Alfred, Lord Tennyson's 'Morte d'Arthur', in *Selected Poems*, selected by Michael Baron (London: Phoenix Poetry, 2002), p. 25

p. 55 Arthur Rimbaud, *Illuminations*, translated by John Ashbery (Manchester: Carcanet, 2011), p. 51

p. 56 Ibid. p. 137

p. 68 Originally published in *Imagined Spaces*, edited by Kirsty Gunn and Gail Low (Dundee: The Voyage Out Press, 2020)

p. 79 John Berger, *The Shape of a Pocket*, p. 89

p. 84 Rainer Maria Rilke, 'Solitude', translated by Jessie Lamont (1918), published in *The Collected Works of Rainer Maria Rilke* (Pergamon Media, 2015)

p. 96 Jorge Luis Borges, *A Universal History of Iniquity*, preface to the 1954 edition, collected in *Jorge Luis Borges: Collected Fictions*, translated by Andrew Hurley (London: Penguin, 1998), p. 5

p. 107 Virginia Woolf, letter to Clive Bell quoted in *Art, Life and Vision*, p. 67

Index

Colophon

Thank you to Ornan, Num and to my editor Mona at
Sylph Editions for our friendship and conversations
over 14 years. To my family and extended family, my
mother and father especially. To friends and colleagues
Kirsty, Simon, Jo, Cara, Alice, Gus, George, Stephen,
Noelle, Elizabeth, Jennie, Gillian, Eric, Joomart,
Lorna, Lemn, Ligang, Baldwin, Venera, Alexander,
Alexandra, Hope, Susan, Chris, Benji, Hans, Donatien,
Michael, Natasha, James, Prospero, Julian, David,
Jeffrey, Jens, Sophie.

Most of all to my children Marley and Leo.

Paths Converge *Infinite Strange Shapes*

Design: Ornan Rotem | Sylph Design
    Set in Sabon, designed by Jan Tschichold, a classic
    modern typeface based on 16th-century models
Editorial: Mona Gainer-Salim
Print: Identity Print, Paddock Wood

SYLPH EDITIONS · London · 2025

ISBN 978-1-909631-49-6
www.sylpheditions.com